math
expressions
Common Core

Dr. Karen C. Fuson

Homework and Remembering Grade K
Volume 2

This material is based upon work supported by the
National Science Foundation
under Grant Numbers
ESI-9816320, REC-9806020, and RED-935373.

Any opinions, findings, and conclusions, or recommendations expressed in this material
are those of the author and do not necessarily reflect the views of the National Science Foundation.

HMH

Printed in the U.S.A.

ISBN 978-1-328-70259-3

10 0928 26 25 24 23 22

4500848078   B C D E F G

Name _____

Fill in the partners to complete the partner equation.

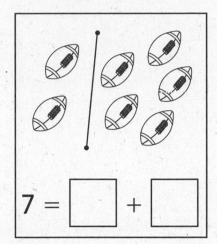

7 = ☐ + ☐

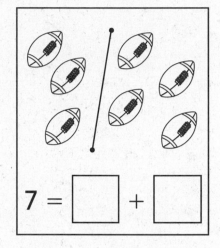

7 = ☐ + ☐

7 = ☐ + ☐

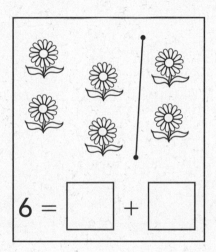

6 = ☐ + ☐

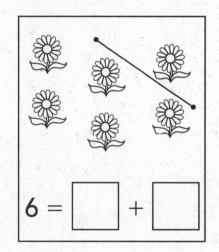

6 = ☐ + ☐

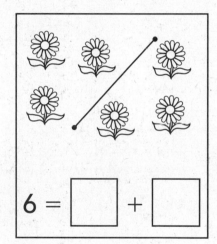

6 = ☐ + ☐

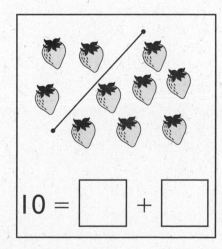

10 = ☐ + ☐

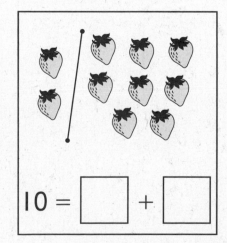

10 = ☐ + ☐

▶ **On the Back** Draw a picture for the equation 7 = 6 + 1.

Name

Draw a line to show the partners. Write the partners.

$10 = \boxed{} + \boxed{}$

$10 = \boxed{} + \boxed{}$

$10 = \boxed{} + \boxed{}$

$10 = \boxed{} + \boxed{}$

$10 = \boxed{} + \boxed{}$

$10 = \boxed{} + \boxed{}$

$10 = \boxed{} + \boxed{}$

$10 = \boxed{} + \boxed{}$

$10 = \boxed{} + \boxed{}$

Draw to show 10 + 2.

Draw to show 10 + 5.

Teen Numbers and Equations

Name _____

Write the partners.

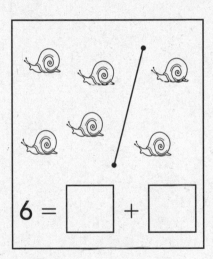

5 = ☐ + ☐

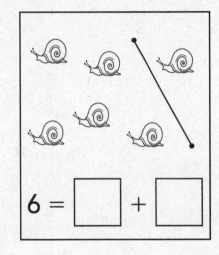

5 = ☐ + ☐

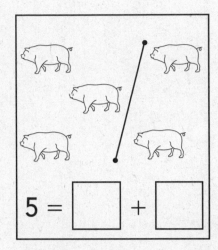

5 = ☐ + ☐

6 = ☐ + ☐

6 = ☐ + ☐

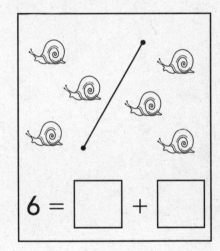

6 = ☐ + ☐

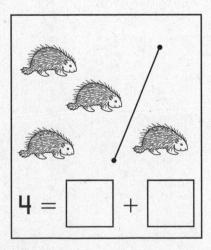

4 = ☐ + ☐

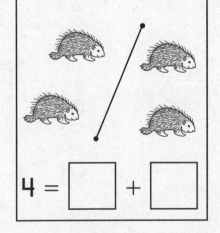

4 = ☐ + ☐

On the Back Draw a picture for the equation 6 = 2 + 4. Draw the Break-Apart Stick.

Addition and Subtraction Stories: Grocery Store Scenario

Name _____

Write the partners.

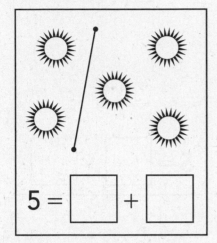

5 = ☐ + ☐

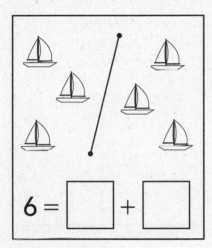

6 = ☐ + ☐

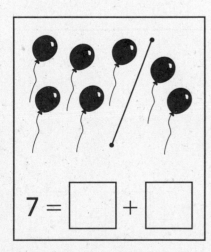

7 = ☐ + ☐

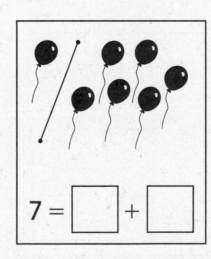

5 = ☐ + ☐

6 = ☐ + ☐

7 = ☐ + ☐

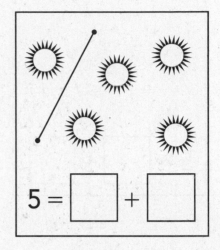

5 = ☐ + ☐

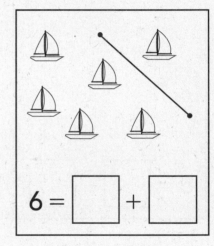

6 = ☐ + ☐

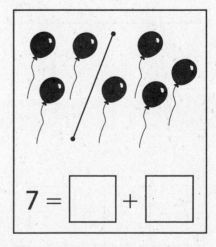

7 = ☐ + ☐

➡ **On the Back** Make your own partner drawings. Write the partners.

$5 = \boxed{} + \boxed{}$

$5 = \boxed{} + \boxed{}$

$5 = \boxed{} + \boxed{}$

$6 = \boxed{} + \boxed{}$

$6 = \boxed{} + \boxed{}$

$6 = \boxed{} + \boxed{}$

$7 = \boxed{} + \boxed{}$

$7 = \boxed{} + \boxed{}$

$7 = \boxed{} + \boxed{}$

Practice Teen Numbers and Equations

Name _____

Draw a line to show two partners. Write the partners.

$6 = \boxed{} + \boxed{}$

$6 = \boxed{} + \boxed{}$

$6 = \boxed{} + \boxed{}$

$5 = \boxed{} + \boxed{}$

$5 = \boxed{} + \boxed{}$

$10 = \boxed{} + \boxed{}$

$10 = \boxed{} + \boxed{}$

$10 = \boxed{} + \boxed{}$

$10 = \boxed{} + \boxed{}$

$10 = \boxed{} + \boxed{}$

$4 = \boxed{} + \boxed{}$ $4 = \boxed{} + \boxed{}$

On the Back Make your own partner drawings for numbers 5, 6, and 7. Write the partners.

$5 = \boxed{} + \boxed{}$

$5 = \boxed{} + \boxed{}$

$5 = \boxed{} + \boxed{}$

$6 = \boxed{} + \boxed{}$

$6 = \boxed{} + \boxed{}$

$6 = \boxed{} + \boxed{}$

$7 = \boxed{} + \boxed{}$

$7 = \boxed{} + \boxed{}$

$7 = \boxed{} + \boxed{}$

Break-Apart Numbers for 10

Name _____

1 Count and write the number. Circle the number that is greater.

(4) 1

☐ ☐

☐ ☐

☐ ☐

☐ ☐

☐ ☐

2 Count and write the number. Circle the number that is less.

☐ ☐

☐ ☐

☐ ☐

☐ ☐

☐ ☐

☐ ☐

3 Write the numbers 1 through 20 in order.

Addition and Subtraction Drawings: Grocery Store Scenario **77**

Name _____

4 Draw lines to match. Circle the extras. Write the numbers and compare them.
Write G for Greater than and L for Less than.

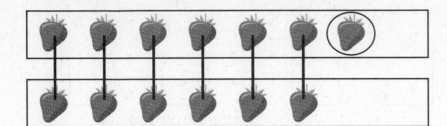

7	G
6	L

□	__
□	__

□	__
□	__

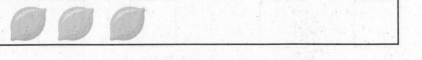

□	__
□	__

□	__
□	__

Addition and Subtraction Drawings: Grocery Store Scenario

Draw Tiny Tumblers on the Math Mountains.

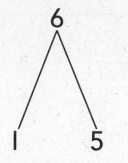 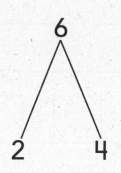 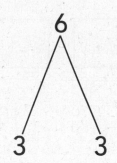 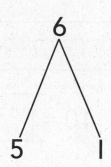 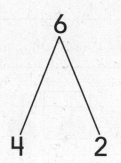

6   6   6   6   6

1 5   2 4   3 3   4 2   5 1

 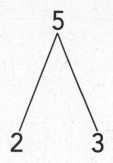 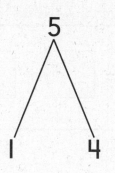 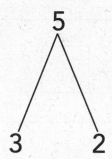 

2   5   5   5   5

1 1   1 4   2 3   3 2   4 1

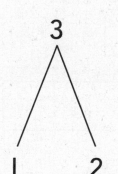 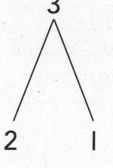   

3   3   4   4   4

1 2   2 1   1 3   2 2   3 1

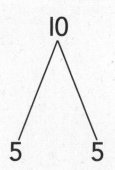 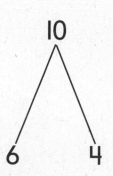 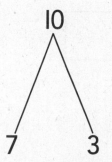 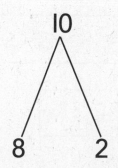 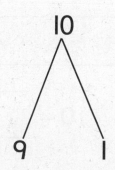

10   10   10   10   10

5 5   6 4   7 3   8 2   9 1

Draw a line to show the partners. Write the partners.

10 = ☐ + ☐   10 = ☐ + ☐

10 = ☐ + ☐   10 = ☐ + ☐

10 = ☐ + ☐   10 = ☐ + ☐

10 = ☐ + ☐   10 = ☐ + ☐

10 = ☐ + ☐

Name _____

Draw Tiny Tumblers on the Math Mountains.

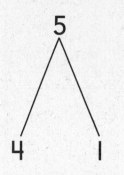
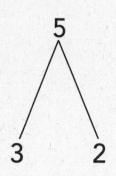
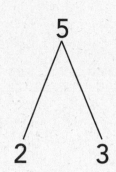

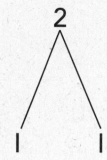

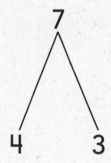
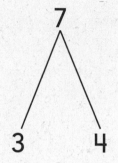
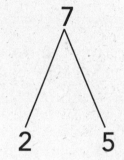

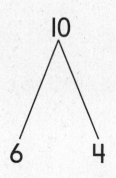

Write the numbers 1 through 20.

➡ **On the Back** Make a picture with squares, circles, triangles, and rectangles.

More Partners of 10 with 5-Groups

1 Draw lines to match.

  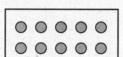  

9

7

10

6

8

2 Make two matches.

4

5

3

2

1

 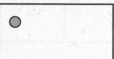 

3 Connect the dots in order.

   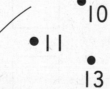 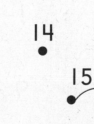  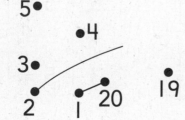 

4 Write the numbers 1 through 20.

5 Add the numbers.

$4 + 1 = \boxed{}$ $2 + 3 = \boxed{}$ $3 + 1 = \boxed{}$

$1 + 3 = \boxed{}$ $3 + 0 = \boxed{}$ $2 + 1 = \boxed{}$

$1 + 2 = \boxed{}$ $2 + 2 = \boxed{}$ $1 + 3 = \boxed{}$

$2 + 3 = \boxed{}$ $3 + 2 = \boxed{}$ $5 + 0 = \boxed{}$

$1 + 5 = \boxed{}$ $1 + 8 = \boxed{}$ $3 + 7 = \boxed{}$

$3 + 4 = \boxed{}$ $9 + 1 = \boxed{}$ $4 + 4 = \boxed{}$

$4 + 3 = \boxed{}$ $5 + 1 = \boxed{}$ $5 + 5 = \boxed{}$

$2 + 7 = \boxed{}$ $6 + 3 = \boxed{}$ $3 + 5 = \boxed{}$

Teen Number Book

Name _____

1 Draw Tiny Tumblers on the Math Mountains.

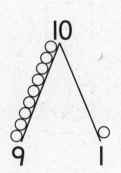
6
5   1

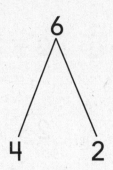
6
4   2

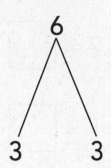
6
3   3

6
2   4

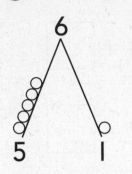
6
1   5

5
4   1

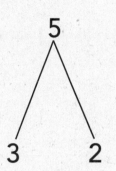
5
3   2

5
2   3

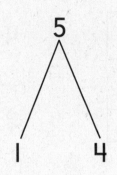
5
1   4

2
1   1

10
9   1

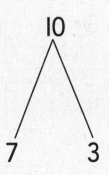
10
8   2

10
7   3

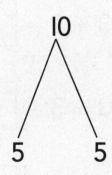
10
6   4

10
5   5

2 Write the numbers 1 through 20.

Name _____

3 Add the numbers.

$4 + 0 = \boxed{}$

$3 + 1 = \boxed{}$

$1 + 3 = \boxed{}$

$1 + 2 = \boxed{}$

$3 + 2 = \boxed{}$

$3 + 3 = \boxed{}$

$2 + 4 = \boxed{}$

$3 + 5 = \boxed{}$

$1 + 5 = \boxed{}$

$2 + 2 = \boxed{}$

$1 + 1 = \boxed{}$

$4 + 1 = \boxed{}$

$2 + 1 = \boxed{}$

$0 + 3 = \boxed{}$

$6 + 4 = \boxed{}$

$3 + 4 = \boxed{}$

$4 + 2 = \boxed{}$

$6 + 3 = \boxed{}$

$2 + 3 = \boxed{}$

$2 + 2 = \boxed{}$

$1 + 0 = \boxed{}$

$1 + 4 = \boxed{}$

$3 + 1 = \boxed{}$

$8 + 2 = \boxed{}$

$6 + 1 = \boxed{}$

$5 + 2 = \boxed{}$

$3 + 7 = \boxed{}$

Addition Equations

Name

1 Add the numbers.

2 + 2 = ☐   0 + 2 = ☐   1 + 2 = ☐

3 + 1 = ☐   1 + 4 = ☐   5 + 0 = ☐

2 + 3 = ☐   4 + 0 = ☐   1 + 3 = ☐

2 + 1 = ☐   0 + 5 = ☐   1 + 1 = ☐

3 + 2 = ☐   4 + 1 = ☐   2 + 3 = ☐

2 Connect the dots in order.

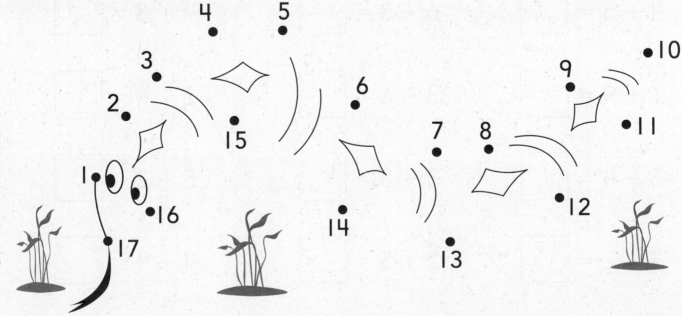

3 Add the numbers.

2 + 2 = ☐   1 + 3 = ☐   5 + 0 = ☐

3 + 0 = ☐   2 + 1 = ☐   4 + 1 = ☐

1 + 4 = ☐   1 + 0 = ☐   1 + 2 = ☐

2 + 3 = ☐   3 + 2 = ☐   4 + 1 = ☐

0 + 4 = ☐   3 + 1 = ☐   1 + 1 = ☐

4 + 5 = ☐   6 + 3 = ☐   4 + 3 = ☐

1 + 9 = ☐   3 + 6 = ☐   2 + 4 = ☐

6 + 4 = ☐   3 + 3 = ☐   5 + 2 = ☐

7 + 2 = ☐   2 + 5 = ☐   4 + 4 = ☐

Write Addition Equations

Name _____

Count the stars. Write the number.

 _____

 _____

 _____

 _____

Count the gray stars. Write the number.
Count the white stars. Write the number.
Write how many stars in all.

_____ + _____ = _____

_____ + _____ = _____

_____ + _____ = _____

_____ + _____ = _____

Partners of 10: Stars in the Night Sky

Name _____

Circle the 10-group in the picture.
Write the equation with a group of tens and more ones.

$\underline{\quad 10 \quad} + \underline{\quad 9 \quad} = \underline{\quad 19 \quad}$

$\underline{\qquad} + \underline{\qquad} = \underline{\qquad}$

$\underline{\qquad} + \underline{\qquad} = \underline{\qquad}$

$\underline{\qquad} + \underline{\qquad} = \underline{\qquad}$

$\underline{\qquad} + \underline{\qquad} = \underline{\qquad}$

$\underline{\qquad} + \underline{\qquad} = \underline{\qquad}$

On the Back Choose a teen number. Draw that number of circles. Make a 10-group.

Solve and Retell Story Problems

Add the numbers. Use your fingers or draw.

4 + 1 = ☐   3 + 3 = ☐   5 + 4 = ☐

3 + 2 = ☐   5 + 3 = ☐   2 + 2 = ☐

2 + 0 = ☐   4 + 2 = ☐   4 + 3 = ☐

5 + 2 = ☐   3 + 1 = ☐   5 + 1 = ☐

2 + 1 = ☐   4 + 0 = ☐   4 + 2 = ☐

Equal or not equal? = or ≠	Equal or not equal? = or ≠	Equal or not equal? = or ≠
3 2 + 1		1 0 + 2
2 2 + 2		3 1 + 2
1 3 + 2		2 2 + 3
4 1 + 3		5 4 + 1
5 3 + 0		4 1 + 2

➡ **On the Back** Write the numbers 1–100.

1	2								10
11									
									100

Numbers 1–100

Circle the 10-group. Write the ten and ones in each equation.

___10___ + ___3___ = ___13___   _____ + _____ = _____

_____ + _____ = _____   _____ + _____ = _____

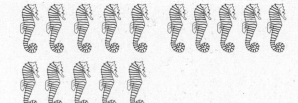

_____ + _____ = _____   _____ + _____ = _____

_____ + _____ = _____   _____ + _____ = _____

_____ + _____ = _____   _____ + _____ = _____

> **On the Back** Make a picture with shapes.

Name _____

Draw Tiny Tumblers on the Math Mountains.

3
1   2

3
2   1

4
3   1

4
2   2

5
4   1

5
3   2
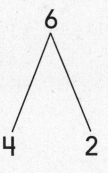

5
1   4
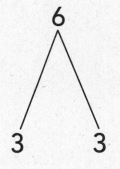

5
2   3

6
5   1
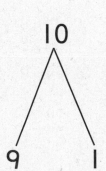

6
4   2

6
3   3
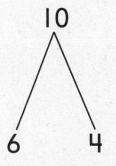

6
2   4

10
9   1

10
7   3

10
6   4

10
5   5

➡ **On the Back** Draw four different Math Mountains for 8.

© Houghton Mifflin Harcourt Publishing Company

Review Partners

Draw circles to show each number.
Write the ten and the ones under the circles.

11	12	13	14	15	16	17	18	19	20
10 + 1	10 +	+	+	+	+	+	10 +	+	+

Complete the equations.

$12 = 10 + \underline{}$ $19 = 10 + \underline{}$ $15 = 10 + \underline{}$

$16 = 10 + \underline{}$ $17 = 10 + \underline{}$ $13 = 10 + \underline{}$

$14 = 10 + \underline{}$ $18 = 10 + \underline{}$

⬆ **On the Back** Add the numbers.

1 + 0 = ☐   2 + 1 = ☐   2 + 3 = ☐

3 + 1 = ☐   2 + 2 = ☐   1 + 1 = ☐

4 + 1 = ☐   1 + 2 = ☐   3 + 2 = ☐

3 + 1 = ☐   1 + 4 = ☐   4 + 1 = ☐

1 + 3 = ☐   4 + 0 = ☐   1 + 2 = ☐

4 + 5 = ☐   3 + 4 = ☐   2 + 8 = ☐

1 + 7 = ☐   3 + 7 = ☐   4 + 4 = ☐

9 + 1 = ☐   8 + 2 = ☐   2 + 7 = ☐

1 + 5 = ☐   5 + 4 = ☐   4 + 2 = ☐

Partners of 6, 7, 8, and 9

Draw Tiny Tumblers on the Math Mountains.
Write the partners.

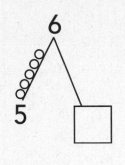
6
5 ☐

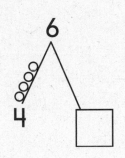
6
4 ☐

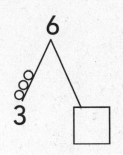
6
3 ☐

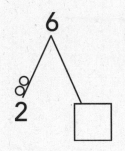
6
2 ☐

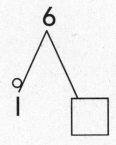
6
1 ☐

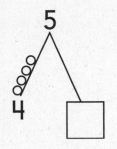
5
4 ☐

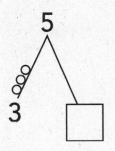
5
3 ☐

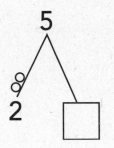
5
2 ☐

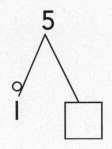
5
1 ☐

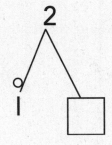
2
1 ☐

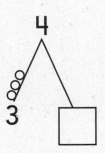
4
3 ☐

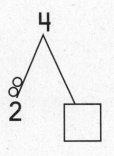
4
2 ☐

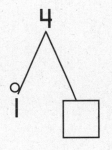
4
1 ☐

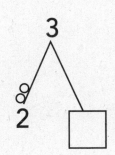
3
2 ☐

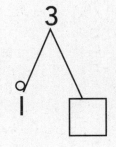
3
1 ☐

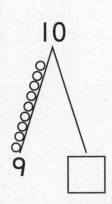
10
9 ☐

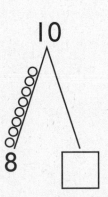
10
8 ☐

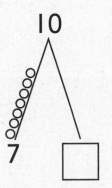
10
7 ☐

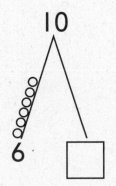
10
6 ☐

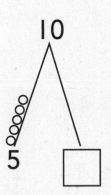
10
5 ☐

▶ **On the Back** Draw four different Math Mountains for 9.

Tens in Teen Numbers: A Game

Think 5-groups to find the totals.
Color each balloon.

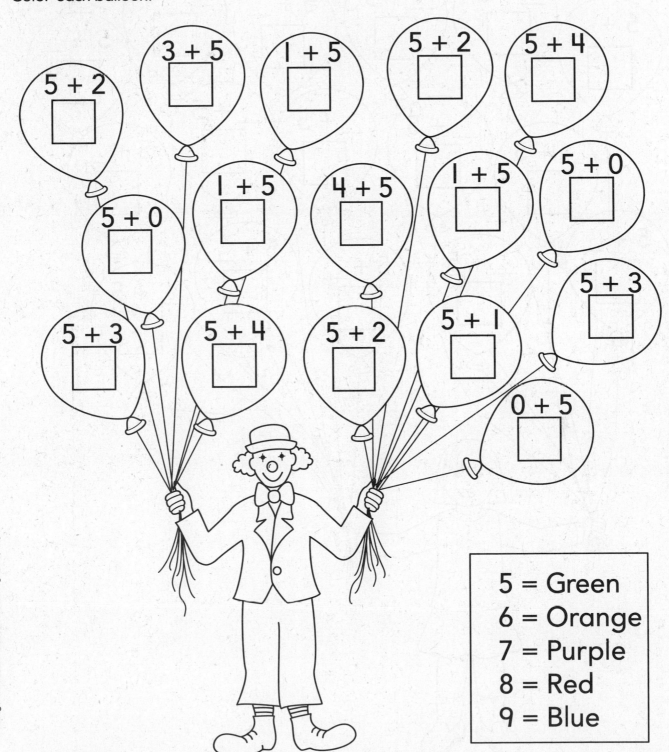

5 = Green
6 = Orange
7 = Purple
8 = Red
9 = Blue

➡ **On the Back** Make and answer your own 5-group problems.

Tens in Teen Numbers Book

Subtract the numbers. Use your fingers or draw.

5 − 1 = ☐   5 − 3 = ☐   4 − 0 = ☐

5 − 2 = ☐   5 − 4 = ☐   2 − 1 = ☐

5 − 0 = ☐   4 − 3 = ☐   4 − 3 = ☐

4 − 2 = ☐   3 − 2 = ☐   5 − 1 = ☐

3 − 1 = ☐   3 − 0 = ☐   5 − 2 = ☐

Write the symbol to show equal or not equal.
     = or ≠

2	≠	0 + 1			5	1 + 4
1		3 + 1			3	2 + 3
3		2 + 1			4	3 + 2
5		2 + 3			1	2 + 1
4		3 + 0			2	0 + 2

🡒 **On the Back** Write the numbers 1–100.

1	11								
2									
10									100

Partners of 10: Class Project

Name _____

Subtract the numbers. Use your fingers or draw.

4 − 1 = ☐   5 − 1 = ☐   4 − 2 = ☐

2 − 2 = ☐   4 − 0 = ☐   5 − 0 = ☐

3 − 0 = ☐   5 − 3 = ☐   4 − 3 = ☐

5 − 2 = ☐   3 − 2 = ☐   2 − 1 = ☐

3 − 1 = ☐   1 − 0 = ☐   5 − 5 = ☐

Write the symbol to show equal or not equal.

= or ≠

           10   2 + 7   8   5 + 3

          6   4 + 2   6   4 + 3

          9   4 + 4   9   2 + 5

          7   2 + 6   7   1 + 6

          8   4 + 3   5   3 + 3

▶ **On the Back** Write the numbers 1–100.

1	2								10
11									
21									
									100

Introduction to Counting and Grouping Routines

Name _____

Draw Tiny Tumblers. Write how many there are on each Math Mountain.

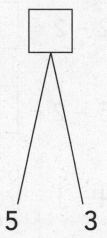

7   1   6   2   5   3   4   4

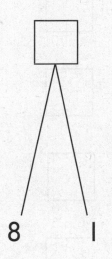

8   1   7   2   6   3   5   4

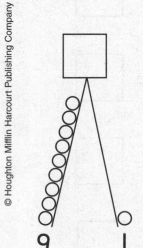
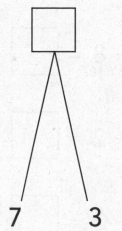

9   1   8   2   7   3   6   4   5   5

⬤➤ **On the Back** Subtract the numbers.

Name _____

Subtract the numbers.

4 − 3 = ☐   2 − 2 = ☐   5 − 1 = ☐

3 − 1 = ☐   5 − 2 = ☐   0 − 0 = ☐

4 − 2 = ☐   4 − 1 = ☐   5 − 3 = ☐

5 − 4 = ☐   3 − 1 = ☐   4 − 0 = ☐

2 − 1 = ☐   1 − 0 = ☐   3 − 3 = ☐

7 − 6 = ☐   8 − 2 = ☐   10 − 7 = ☐

8 − 4 = ☐   9 − 6 = ☐   7 − 2 = ☐

10 − 5 = ☐   9 − 8 = ☐   8 − 3 = ☐

8 − 5 = ☐   6 − 2 = ☐   7 − 4 = ☐

10 − 8 = ☐   9 − 3 = ☐   10 − 6 = ☐

Add Partners to Find Totals

Name _____

Write the numbers and compare them.
Write G for **Greater** and L for **Less**.
Cross out to make the groups **equal**.

1 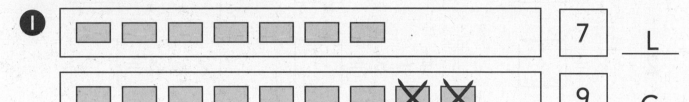 7 L

9 G

2 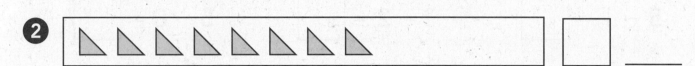 [ ] ___

[ ] ___

3 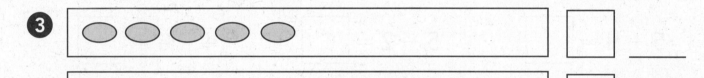 [ ] ___

[ ] ___

4 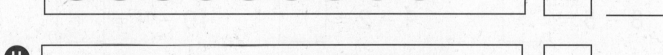 [ ] ___

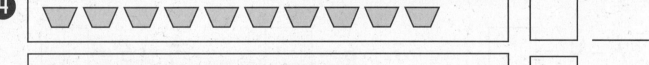 [ ] ___

5 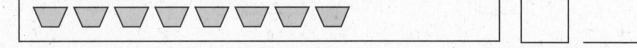 [ ] ___

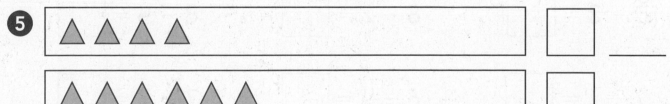 [ ] ___

➡ **On the Back** Subtract the numbers.

Name _____

Subtract the numbers.

$4 - 2 = \square$ $3 - 1 = \square$ $5 - 3 = \square$

$2 - 1 = \square$ $4 - 3 = \square$ $2 - 2 = \square$

$5 - 1 = \square$ $3 - 2 = \square$ $5 - 0 = \square$

$4 - 1 = \square$ $3 - 0 = \square$ $5 - 3 = \square$

$5 - 4 = \square$ $5 - 2 = \square$ $4 - 4 = \square$

$8 - 5 = \square$ $9 - 2 = \square$ $10 - 4 = \square$

$7 - 4 = \square$ $7 - 6 = \square$ $9 - 6 = \square$

$10 - 3 = \square$ $8 - 2 = \square$ $8 - 4 = \square$

$7 - 1 = \square$ $6 - 4 = \square$ $7 - 5 = \square$

$10 - 7 = \square$ $9 - 3 = \square$ $10 - 6 = \square$

Story Problems and Comparing: Totals Through 10

Subtract the numbers.

3 – 2 = ☐   5 – 2 = ☐   8 – 4 = ☐

2 – 1 = ☐   3 – 1 = ☐   6 – 2 = ☐

5 – 1 = ☐   8 – 1 = ☐   4 – 0 = ☐

4 – 4 = ☐   9 – 3 = ☐   9 – 1 = ☐

10 – 1 = ☐   5 – 3 = ☐   4 – 2 = ☐

6 – 4 = ☐   7 – 2 = ☐   2 – 2 = ☐

7 – 4 = ☐   9 – 4 = ☐   6 – 1 = ☐

10 – 4 = ☐   6 – 1 = ☐   10 – 2 = ☐

7 – 3 = ☐   6 – 5 = ☐   8 – 2 = ☐

On the Back Draw two equal groups of triangles.

Subtract to Make Equal Groups